FOLLOW YOUR DREAMS THEY KNOW THE WAY

TEEN
INSPIRATIONAL
COLORING BOOKS

▲ ART THERAPY COLORING

MW01257678

Preview of Coloring Pages

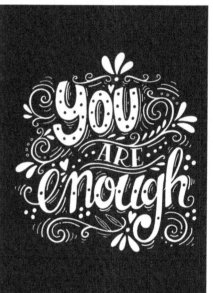

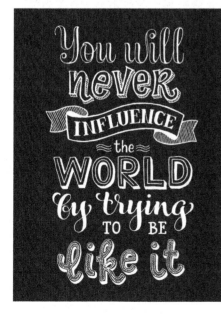

TODAY IS THE DAY

PEOPLE are PRETTIEST WHEN they talk ABOUT something THEY really LOVE

Doubt kills more DREAMS than failure Ever will

Simple is Beautiful

THE PAIN YOU FEEL TODAY IS THE STRENGTH YOU FEEL TOMORROW

YOU are Stronger THAN YOU THINK

LOVE ALL YOU NEED IS

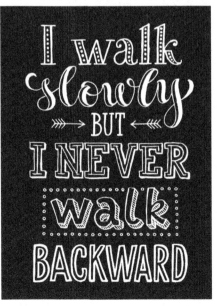

I walk slowly BUT I NEVER walk BACKWARD

DO ALL things WITH kindness

Did You Enjoy Our Coloring Book?

We Want To Hear About It!

Help spread the word about our coloring books! We give 10% of all proceeds from Art Therapy products to benefit cancer patients and their families.

The best way to spread the word is through reviews. We know how busy you are, especially with all of that coloring, but we would appreciate it!

Visit our website at **www.arttherapycoloring.com**

Don't BE AFRAID ... TO BE - GREAT

You will never never INFLUENCE the WORLD by trying TO BE like it

Do more of what makes you AWESOME

You are loved.

EVERYTHING STARTS WITH A dream

Even the DARKEST NIGHT WILL END AND THE SUN will rise

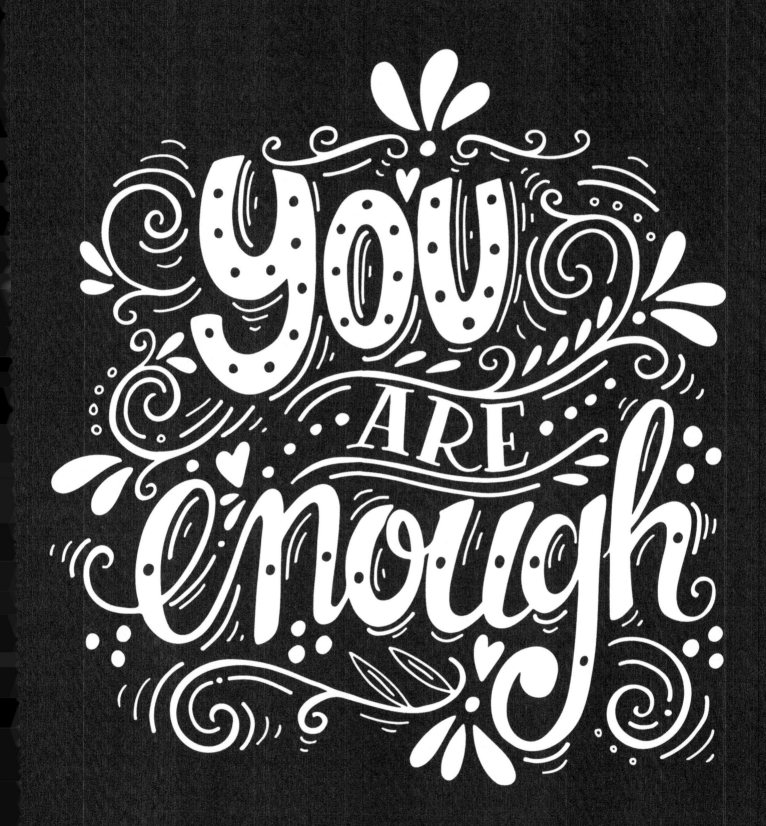

BE COURAGEOUS. FOLLOW THE WONDERS WITH WILL. BE MOTION.

IT ALWAYS SEEMS IMPOSSIBLE UNTIL IT'S DONE

BE THE REASON THAT SOMEONE Smiles TODAY

PEOPLE are
PRETTIEST
WHEN they
talk ABOut
something
THEY
Really
LOVE
♥

Simple is Beautiful

I walk
slowly
BUT →←
I NEVER
walk
BACKWARD

Doubt kills more DREAMS than failure ever will

Visit our website at www.arttherapycoloring.com

Get a Free Printable Coloring Ebook!

We've created an exclusive offer for our customers to receive a free Adult Coloring Ebook.

Visit **www.arttherapycoloring.com/freebie** to claim your free coloring book with over 30 new designs that you can instantly print and color!

Over 100 Art Therapy Coloring Books

See our collection of over 100 Art Therapy Coloring Books for Adults, Men, Women, Seniors, Teens, Kids, Boys, and Girls on the following pages.

Coloring Books For Teens

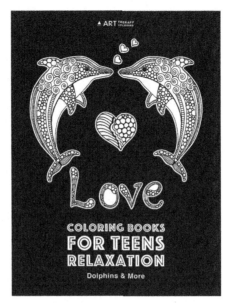

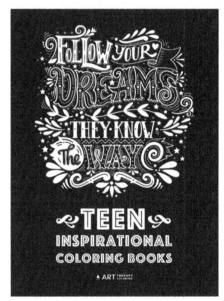

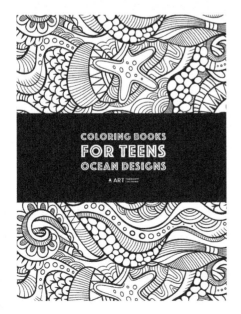

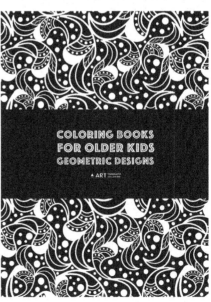

Coloring Books For Teens

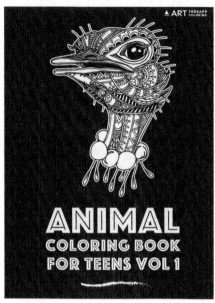

ANIMAL COLORING BOOK FOR TEENS VOL 1

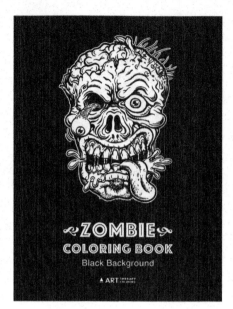

~ZOMBIE~ COLORING BOOK Black Background

SKULL COLORING BOOK FOR TEENS Black Background

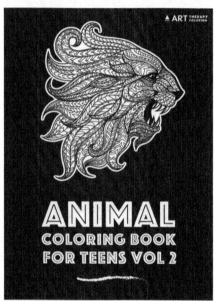

ANIMAL COLORING BOOK FOR TEENS VOL 2

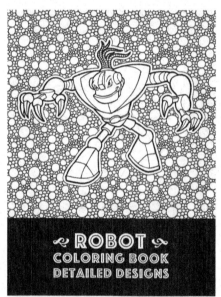

~ROBOT~ COLORING BOOK DETAILED DESIGNS

COLORING BOOKS FOR TEENS WOLVES & MORE

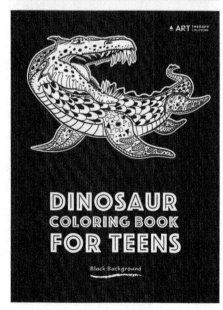

DINOSAUR COLORING BOOK FOR TEENS Black Background

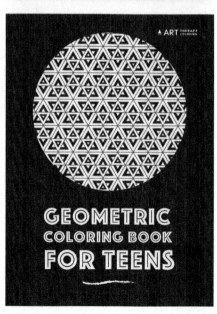

GEOMETRIC COLORING BOOK FOR TEENS

COLORING BOOKS FOR TEENS SHARKS & MORE

Coloring Books For Teens

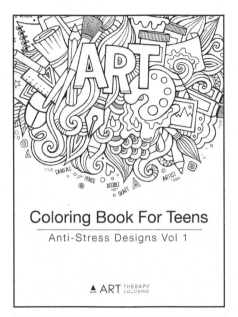

Coloring Book For Teens
Anti-Stress Designs Vol 1

▲ ART THERAPY COLORING

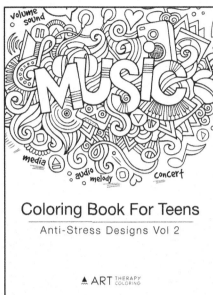

Coloring Book For Teens
Anti-Stress Designs Vol 2

▲ ART THERAPY COLORING

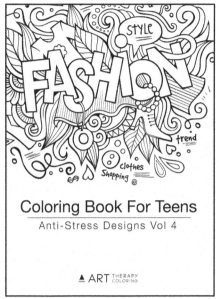

Coloring Book For Teens
Anti-Stress Designs Vol 4

▲ ART THERAPY COLORING

Coloring Book For Teens
Anti-Stress Designs Vol 5

▲ ART THERAPY COLORING

Coloring Book For Teens
Anti-Stress Designs Vol 6

▲ ART THERAPY COLORING

Coloring Book For Teens
Anti-Stress Designs Vol 7

▲ ART THERAPY COLORING

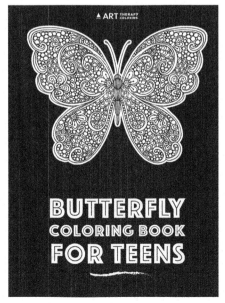

BUTTERFLY COLORING BOOK FOR TEENS

Coloring Book For Teens
Anti-Stress Designs Vol 8

▲ ART THERAPY COLORING

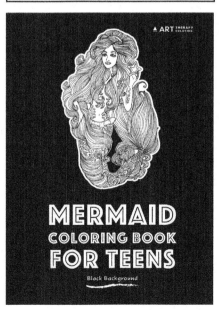

MERMAID COLORING BOOK FOR TEENS
Black Background

Coloring Books For Girls

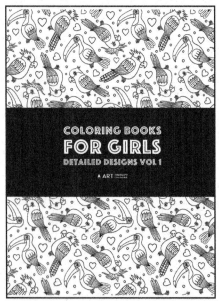

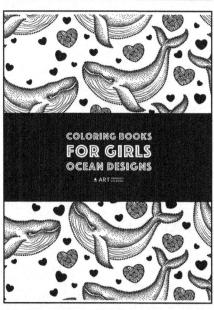

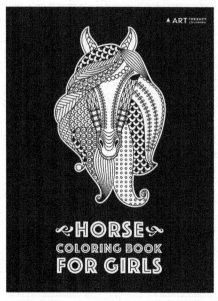

Coloring Books For Kids

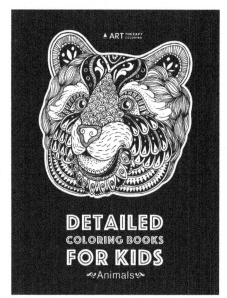

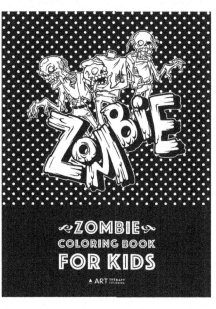

Coloring Books For Boys

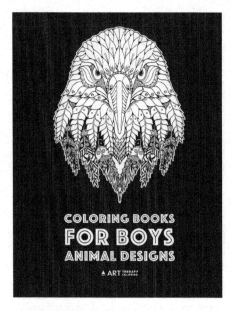

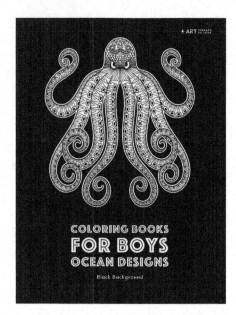

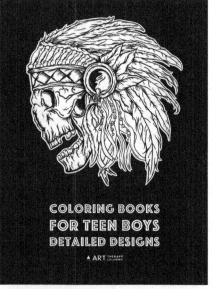

Coloring Books For Men

COLORING BOOK
FOR MEN
ANIMAL DESIGNS

COLORING BOOK
FOR MEN
HAPPY BIRTHDAY
Black Background

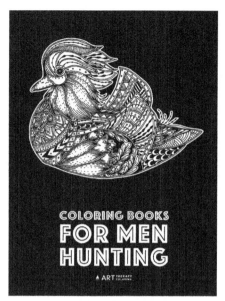

COLORING BOOKS
FOR MEN
HUNTING

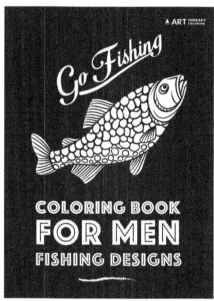

COLORING BOOK
FOR MEN
FISHING DESIGNS

SKULL
COLORING BOOK
FOR ADULTS

FISHING
COLORING BOOK
FOR ADULTS
Black Background

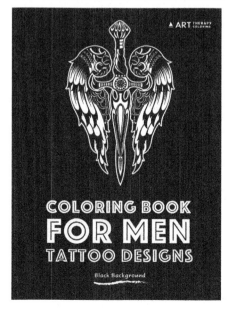

COLORING BOOK
FOR MEN
TATTOO DESIGNS
Black Background

COLORING BOOK
FOR MEN
BIKER DESIGNS

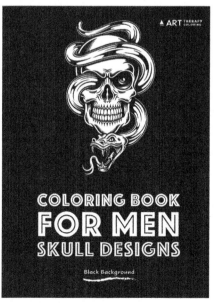

COLORING BOOK
FOR MEN
SKULL DESIGNS
Black Background

Coloring Books For Adults

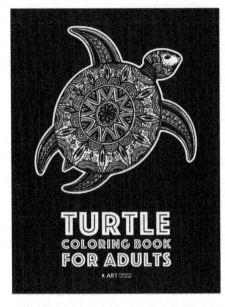

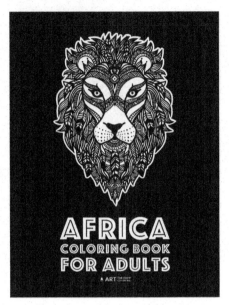

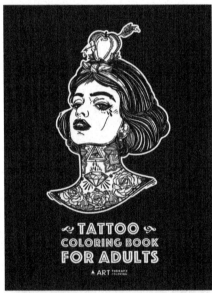

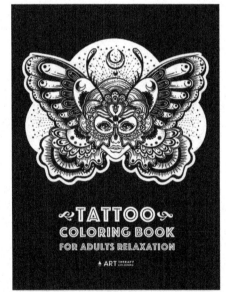

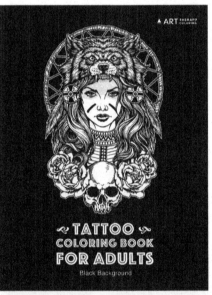

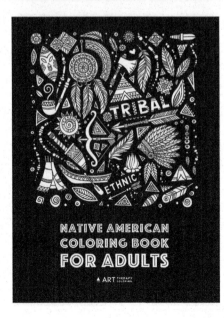

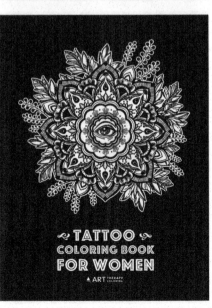

Coloring Books For Adults

Coloring Books For Seniors

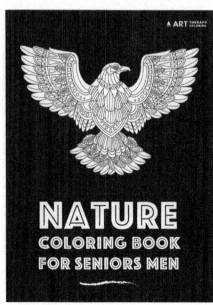

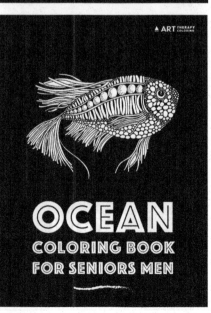

Coloring Books For Special Occasions

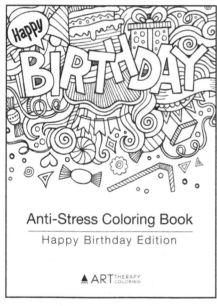

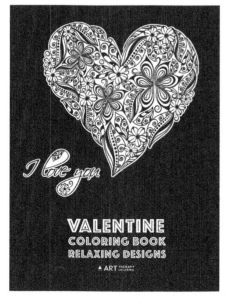

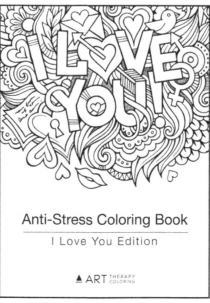

Coloring Books For Christmas

Teen Inspirational Coloring Books

Published by:
Art Therapy Coloring
El Dorado Hills, California
www.arttherapycoloring.com

Copyright © 2017 by Art Therapy Coloring
All Rights Reserved

Shutterstock Images

ISBN: 978-1-64126-096-1

CPSIA information can be obtained
at www.ICGtesting.com
Printed in the USA
BVOW04s1659191217
503199BV00025B/327/P